KNOW THE MARKETS

Tanu Rishi, CFA

”

In the long run, it's not just how much money you make that will determine your future prosperity. It's how much of that money you put to work by saving it and investing it.

- Peter Lynch
GOAT of Investing

PREFACE

It was a Friday dinner night with my friends at a bustling New York City restaurant catching up on how our week went. While we have had numerous such dinners and hundreds of such conversations, this is the one I will never forget. "I am investing $100k in the stock of company X", said one of us. "What?!, Why?!, Don't do it," I quipped, knowing that the amount represents over 25% of my friends' portfolio. I was not even slightly interested to learn the name of the company. My friend invested anyway and incurred heavy losses in a short time. Seven years later, the money is yet to be recovered.

This event is less of a testament to my foresight and more telling of a common issue: people, including highly educated, intelligent, and smart ones, do not understand how the financial markets work. And when I say people, I mean even those who work in the financial industry.

There is research on both sides - supporting that learning about money management does help people make better decisions and the other that claims teaching financial literacy has no material impact on society. I am a firm believer that getting educated most certainly helps one make better decisions. I can affirm from my journey that it was nothing but the knowledge that helped me build my wealth. We may not make all the right choices at all times, but I see zero downsides of knowing the implications of my financial decisions on my future.

With that said, I also acknowledge this is not the most exciting topic to learn out there, but it is one of the most important ones. With this book, I hope to create a fun learning experience and make concepts easy to understand by breaking them down into easy-to assimilate parts. The book covers foundational materials on which you can continue to build on. Money management is lifelong, and reinforcement is critical. I hope this book will provide the framework you need to attain financial happiness.

Happy Investing!

TABLE OF CONTENTS

01

UNDERSTANDING BONDS

What is an Asset Class?

Let's start by defining an asset class. An asset class is defined as a group of financial instruments with similar characteristics.

The two most popular types of asset classes are stocks and bonds. In this lesson, we will learn all about bonds.

What are Bonds?

Bonds are a way through which an institution borrows money. When you buy a bond, you lend money to the institution. If you buy one bond worth $1,000, you are lending that $1,000 of principal in exchange for interest payments.

When you buy a US Treasury bond, you are lending money to the government, say to pay for a new military fighter jet.

If you buy a corporate bond, you lend money to that company to expand its operations.

In return, you receive interest. The interest rate on a bond is also called the coupon of a bond.

Companies and governments issue bonds for a fixed period, at the end of which the institution will return your principal. The coupon (interest rate) and maturity (how long the bond will pay interest) are decided at the time of bond issuance.

What determines a Bond's Coupon?

Conceptually, when an investor loans the money to a company, they will expect the coupon to be in line with the company's creditworthiness.

A stable company with a successful track record is likely to pay your loan back, is thus less risky. The lender will be happy with a low coupon.

However, a new or unstable company has a higher probability of failure, is thus riskier, and will have to pay a higher coupon to compensate the lender for higher risk.

This is similar to when people with higher credit scores get loans at a better interest rate than people with lower credit scores. If someone is to buy either a bond of Apple that pays 3% or the bond of a brand new company that also yields 3%, which bond do you think is better? - Apple, of course. Now, if this 'new' company will pay 10% for the additional risk, one might consider the trade-off.

How do you know if a company is stable?

Here is where the rating agencies like S&P, Moody's, and Fitch do the job for us. Rating agencies will study companies and assign credit ratings similar to how we receive our credit scores. The rating determines if the company can pay not only the interest but also return the borrowed principal at the end of the term. In our example, Apple will get a rating of AAA, and the 'New' company may be rated somewhere in the Bs. The higher the rating, the more stable or creditworthy a company is.

Risk and return of investing in a Bond

When we buy the bond, we get paid a fixed interest - then what is the risk?

Let's look at how you can make or lose money on Bonds other than interest payments. Assume you bought an Apple bond in 2021 for $100 (this is the principal you lend to the company), paying a 3% coupon (this is the interest rate company will pay you), maturing in 15 years (this is how long you will receive interest). Apple agrees to pay you 3% as the market interest rates are 3% or else no one will buy the bond.

Year 2021 → Interest rates in the market = 3% → You buy Apple bond for $100 paying 3% interest

Year 2022 → Interest rates in the market = 4% → Your Apple bond will sell for less than $100

OR

Year 2022 → Interest rates in the market = 2% → Your Apple bond will sell for more than $100

Now we are in the year 2022. Market rates go up, say to 4%.if Apple issues more bonds in 2022 - the new bonds will pay 4% as the overall market rates have increased. In this scenario, your 2021 Apple bond is paying a lower interest than the new 2022 bond - making your bond inferior. Hence, the price of your bond will have to decrease if you want to get a buyer interested.

Alternatively, if the market rates dropped to 2%, your Apple bond will increase in price. Your bond is paying better interest than the 2022 bond, so is a better deal and hence will fetch a higher price.

In addition to the risk of a change in the price of the bond due to changes in market rates, there is also a risk to your principal if the company goes bankrupt and is unable to pay back its loan. So now you know how what to consider when investing in a bond (price of the bond, market interest rates, and stability of the company).

So now you see how you can make or lose money on the bonds as the interest rates in the market change or the company becomes insolvent. Your bonds can also gain or lose value due to other factors like rating changes. A downgrade in rating will cause the bonds to drop in price.

Why invest in Bonds?

Like any other assets, bonds have risks but can also be a good investment vehicle. Following are the reasons why bonds can be a good investment vehicle:

1. Provides a stable income throughout the life of the bond and preserves principal. So they are a good option for near-retirees or retirees

2. When interest rates in the market drop, bonds can perform better than stocks because of an increase in their prices

3. They provide diversification benefits, more on this later.

That was all the Bond basics. Stay on to learn about Stocks.

Bonds

QUIZ

1. What are bonds?

A. Ownership of an institution
B. Loan given to an institution
C. Option to buy the institution in the future

2. What is the coupon of a bond?

A. Price of buying a bond
B. Discount on the price of the bond
C. Interest % that you receive when you buy a bond

3. Which of the following are credit rating agencies?

A. Moody's
B. S&P
C. Both

4. What is the credit rating of a bond?

A. It shows how good the institution will be to return the loan principal. The higher the rating, the less risky the company is
B. It shows how good the institution will be to return the loan principal. The higher the rating, the more risky the company is
C. Credit rating does not apply to bonds but only applies to individuals

5. Who should typically invest in bonds?

A. People who are investing for the first time
B. Retirees or people nearing retirement
C. Anyone in their 30s

1.B | 2.C | 3.C | 4.A | 5.B

02

UNDERSTANDING STOCKS

Stocks, also known as equities, are the most popular asset class. Technology advancements have made trading easy for everyone, which is excellent news. However, the risks of investment have not changed much. Let's learn more about Stocks.

What is a Stock?

Stocks are how an institution raises money to undertake projects for future growth. When you buy a company's stock, you become a shareholder or the owner of the company, in proportion to the size of your investment.

If you buy a sizable number of shares, you even get to influence the company's decisions.

How do you make money on stocks?

Stocks do not pay any interest like bonds. The returns on stock investments primarily come from two sources:

1. Dividends - When a company makes a profit, it gets shared with the business owners as dividends. As a stockholder, you are one of the owners; hence you receive dividends.
2. Price Appreciation - An increase in the stock price due to continued success and positive growth outlook for the company

Remember, unless you sell your stocks, the stock price gains are only on paper (i.e., unrealized gains), unlike the dividends, which are actual payments.

The company can sometimes choose not to pay out the profits but rather invest these profits back in the business for future growth. Not paying dividends is not necessarily bad; because if the company has good products and is well run, your return will eventually show up either in future dividends or in the form of an increased stock price.

How is the price of a stock determined?

Most simplistically, the stock price is expected future profits of the company in today's terms, divided by the number of stocks. If the company performs well and projects growth in its earnings, the stock price will appreciate reflecting this expected growth.

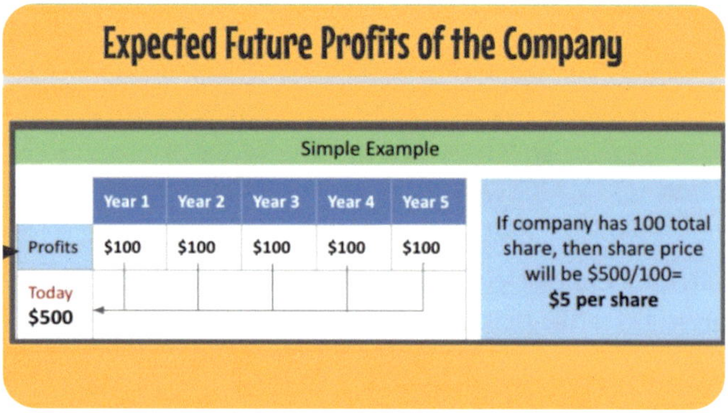

How do you know if the price is right?

This part is more complicated than you think. Numerous other factors contribute to stock price determination in the real world, but ultimately it all boils down to a good product and a well-run company. After performing the necessary analysis, an investor would buy a stock if he believes that he will get his "expected" growth of his investment.

P/E ratio & what it means for the price

You also hear terms like undervalued and overvalued. If an investor thinks that the stock's current price should be higher based on how the company's future appears to be, they will consider the stock undervalued. On the other hand, if the investors assess that the prospects are not as rosy as the stock price reflects, the stock is then categorized as overvalued.

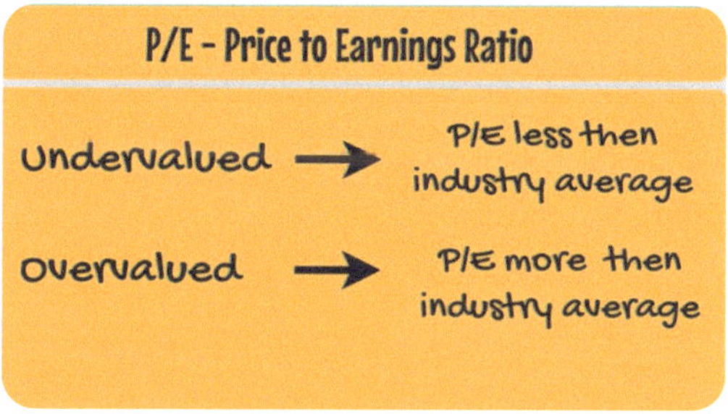

We often hear the team P/E thrown around in this context. The Price upon Earnings ratio indicates how long it will take for you to recoup your investments. A P/E higher than the industry average makes a stock overvalued and lower, undervalued. However, P/E is not the sole determinant. Like we mentioned, many factors go into analyzing the appeal of a stock.

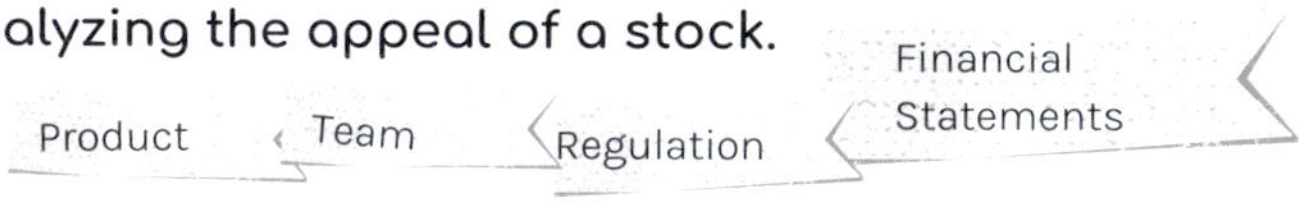

The key learning is that stock at $10 or $1000 does not mean anything by itself unless you consider future profits and other valuation factors. The $10 stock can be overvalued, and a $1000 stock can very well be undervalued.

What are the Risks?

Stock is an ownership in a piece of the company. As the company does well, so does the stock, but if it goes the other way, you not only do not get any dividends, but you also start to lose your principal. If someone is to ask how much money do I stand to lose? The answer will be 100%.

Of course, it's not all that bleak; many well-run companies are great investment options. The challenge is mainly to identify the correct ones and practice discipline. It is nearly impossible for an everyday investor to keep analyzing stocks, not to mention the depth and knowledge needed to do so. You can hire advisors to manage your money or do it yourself using index funds.

Investing in any investment product, including Stocks, depends on your risk tolerance, age, and investment goals.

What are your actual (net) returns on stocks?

Now let's turn to a topic that is not that popular when people talk about stock investments. Two things significantly reduce your returns on stocks:

Taxes eat into your return and can be a significant drag on the returns coupled with the compounding effect. Dividends are taxed at the same rate as your income tax bracket. Due to this reason, sometimes investors prefer stocks that pay low dividends in return for higher growth in the stock prices. Gains on selling stocks sold after more than one year of purchase are taxed at a lower rate vs. ones sold within one year.

Nevertheless, if you keep buying and selling a lot, this can significantly drag your return over long periods.

Example

If you made $100 on your $1000 investment and your tax bracket is 25%, you are left with just $75 in profits. Taxes can have tremendous implications on your money's long-term growth over a 30-40 year investment horizon.

If you sell your stock that has gained value after one year of holding, you will pay a long-term gains tax rate typically lower than a short-term (less than one year) taxable rate.

Fees are charged every quarter and can come in the form of expense ratio, advisory fees, custodian fees, trading fees, load fees, to name a few. The famous 2/20 hedge fund fee means that a hedge fund will charge you 2% advisory fees a year on the money you invest and another 20% on all the gains. Fees similar to taxes can significantly impact your investment returns.

This wraps up Stock basics. Take the quiz to test your knowledge.

Stocks

QUIZ

1. What are Stocks?

A. Part ownership of an institution
B. Loan given to an institution
C. Option to buy the institution in the future

2. What is the dividend of a Stock?

A. Price of buying a Stock
B. Profits shared by the company with shareholders
C. Interest % that you receive for buying the stock

3. Which of the following can impact your returns on investment?

A. Taxes
B. Fees
C. Both

4. Dividends are taxed at?

A. Short term taxable rates
B. Your income tax bracket rate
C. Long term taxable rates

5. In the simplest way, the stock price is?

A. Value of a company's future profits in today's terms
B. Set by the company every year
C. Set by brokers

1.A | 2.B | 3.C | 4.B | 5.A

03

UNDERSTANDING INDEXES

When you hear the statement like the S&P is up or the DOW is down - what does that mean? Let's break it down.

What are Indexes?

An index is a basket of securities, which is nothing more than a collection of similarly characterized financial instruments that fall under some predetermined parameters.

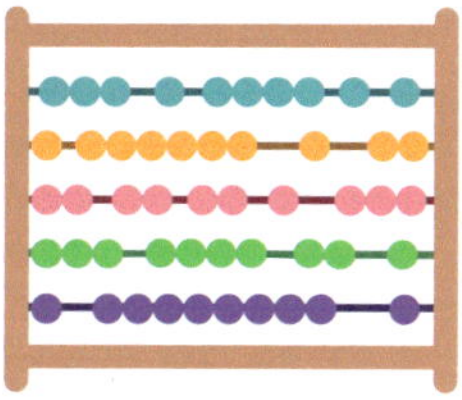

For example, the S&P 500 index consists of the 500 largest U.S. companies measured by market capitalization.

Market Capitalization =
Stock price x Total number of company stocks

What are Index Funds?

The index funds are investment vehicles that mimic their investments by buying precisely the same securities as the chosen index.

How do you make money with Index Funds?

As the stock price of companies within the index goes up and down, the value of the index increases and decreases. There are technical aspects that pertain to valuing each index. We won't overcomplicate by going into those complexities but instead review a simple example to explain the concept equally well.

There are 500 stocks in the index, each priced at $1 on February 1st. The value of 1 share of the index will be $500. Say you bought one share in S&P 500 index and paid that $500.

Next day half the stocks in the index increased by 10 cents, and half decreased by 5 cents.

<u>500 shares in the Index</u>

Feb 1st	→	1 share of Index = $500 (500 shares X $1))
Feb 2nd	→	1 share of Index = $512.50 (250 shares X $1.10 and ↑ 250 share X .$95) ↓
Gain/Loss	→	**$512.50-$500 = $12.50**

The new value of your one share will be the previous day's value plus/minus the gains or loss. In our example, the new value of the index is $512.50, and your profit is $12.50.

This is how you make profit and loss investing in an index, and this is what investing in an index fund is. Our example only covered a US stock-based index; however, there are thousands of indexes based on different countries, asset classes, and even industries.

To give you more context, below is the composition of the S&P 500 index fund in Dec 2020. So your $500 will be invested in all these companies when you buy one share of an S&P 500 index fund.

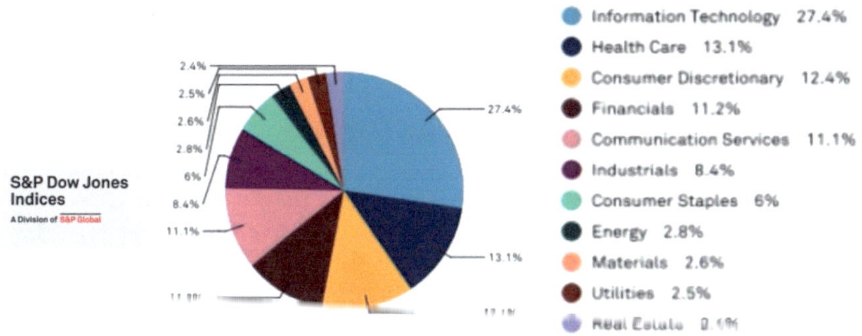

What is active vs passive investing?

Index investing is also called passive investing which aims to reduce frequent buying and selling of stocks. Index funds only buy when a stock is added and only sell when a stock is removed from an index, thereby fully mimicking a specific index.

Exchange Traded Funds or ETFs are a great way to invest in Indexes

ETFs tracks an index, sector, commodity, or other assets

ETFs trade like a stock throughout the day, whereas traditional index funds trade once a day.

On the other hand, active investing involves picking securities, often taking advantage of the short-term market changes, to make better returns than the index. Typically, portfolio managers engage in stock selection and active money management.

You can invest in this strategy using Mutual funds.

Actively managed by fund managers and will hold a few to a few hundred stocks.

High trading volume; buy based on changing markets

Some key points in active vs. passive investing choices before we wrap up this chapter:

Preference : LOW FEES	Preference : LOW TAXES	Preference : HIGH RETURNS
BUY ETF	BUY ETF	HIRE PORTFOLIO MANAGER
If you are sensitive to what fees you pay, you should go with index funds or ETF due to their ultra-low fee structure.	If you also are sensitive to tax liability, you should go with ETFs as ETFs are more tax-efficient.	If you believe that having a portfolio manager will provide you better returns after taxes and fees, you can go with Mutual Funds.

History tells us that it is nearly impossible to beat the market over long periods. The extraordinary rise of index funds is a result of these findings.

Indexes

QUIZ

1. What is an Index?

A. Collection of loans
B. Collection of gold bars
C. Collection of securities with similar characteristics

2. What is the market capitalization of a company?

A. Total number of bonds X Bond price
B. Total number of company stocks X Stock Price
C. Interest % that you receive when you buy a bond

3. What is an Index Fund?

A. Funds for retirees
B. A fund that mimics an index by holding the same securities as the specific index
C. Funds for millennials

4. What are ETFs?

A. Executable Trade Futures
B. Way to buy a single stock for free
C. Electronically Traded Funds that can be used for index investing

5. What is passive investing?

A. Buy securities and never sell
B. A way of investing that aims to reduce buying and selling and holding securities for the long term to maximize returns
C. Minimize investing and keeping most of the money in cash

1.C | 2.B | 3.B | 4.C | 5.B

04

UNDERSTANDING RISK VS. RETURN

Why do returns vary?

Have you ever wondered why a company's bond pays higher interest than a bank's cash deposit? This is because bank deposits have certain safeguards to protect consumers as required by the government regulations. The government does not provide similar protections for corporate bonds.

If the bank goes down, the regulatory safeguards will protect you from losses, but if the company whose bonds you purchased goes bankrupt, you stand to lose a lot more than just your interest.

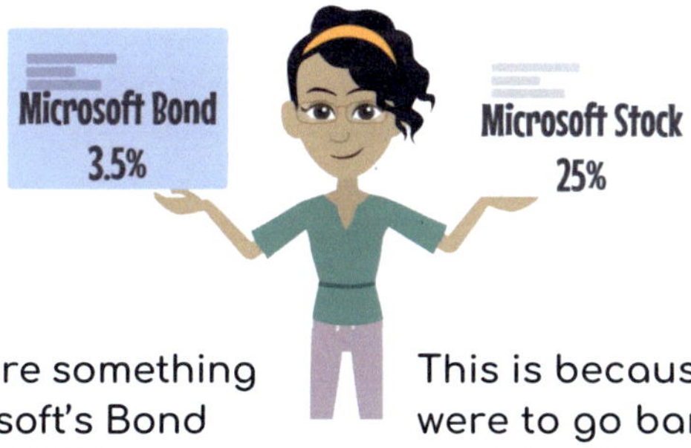

Let's compare something else - Microsoft's Bond pays about 3.5% interest, whereas returns on Microsoft's stock for the past ten years are about 25%. Why?!?

This is because if Microsoft were to go bankrupt, you would still recover at least some of your bond investment as bondholders get paid from the sale of company assets, whereas your stock will be worth zero.

So we can see a pattern here. The return of an investment is directly related to how much risk it carries for it to lose money.

Risk is measured using volatility which is defined as how often and how much the price of a security goes up and down. That is why you hear cryptocurrency is very volatile or risky because the price swings dramatically.

Volatility in price makes an investment risky

Risk is a necessity

The presence of risk does not mean that you should stop investing. Without risk, there is no return. However, a fundamental understanding of the quality of risk that you are taking is essential. Hence, it would be best to establish the level of risk where you would like to invest your money, also known as your risk tolerance. Let's take a look at how.

Risk tolerance is both **psychological** and **situational.**

You should assess how much risk you are willing to take, which is psychological, and how much risk you can take, which is situational. When the two do not align, people often take on investments outside their 'risk tolerance'. This often results in unwanted investment outcomes.

Willingness is defined by your will to accept a loss, and ability is the size of your wealth that will allow for a loss. These two need to be in sync to define your risk tolerance.

Willingness To take risk	Your will to accept a loss →
Ability To take risk	Size of your wealth that will allow for a loss →

If your willingness to take risks is high, and so is your ability, you have an above-average risk tolerance. Meaning, you can invest in high-risk investments for an expected higher return, but you can also absorb higher losses if they do occur.

Defining your risk tolerance

The table summarizes four ways you can define your willingness and ability to take risk. Notice the two problem areas, A and B. 'A' is an issue because you are willing to take high risks, but you cannot afford to absorb the losses. Losses in such a case will most likely cause financial pain. On the contrary, if you are not willing to take risks even though you can despite your wealth (box B), you may miss lucrative investments. Both these instances call for reconciling your willingness and ability for risk, especially box (A). You cannot afford to take unreasonable risks with your investments.

Willingness To take risk	High	High	Low	Low
Ability To take risk	High	Low	High	Low
Risk Tolerance	Above Average	(A) !	(B) !	Below Average

!Reconciliation Needed!

Establishing your return expectations

Now let's turn to the return. Once you have identified your risk tolerance, your return expectation should align with it.

Willingness To take risk	High	Low	Low
Ability To take risk	High	Low	High
Risk Tolerance	Above Average	Average	Average
Expected Return	Above Average	Average	Average

Recall how we mentioned that you cannot expect returns without risk, and higher the risk, higher the returns, and vice versa. Understanding this should make it very easy to identify the return you can anticipate based on your risk tolerance.

Risk and Return are relative

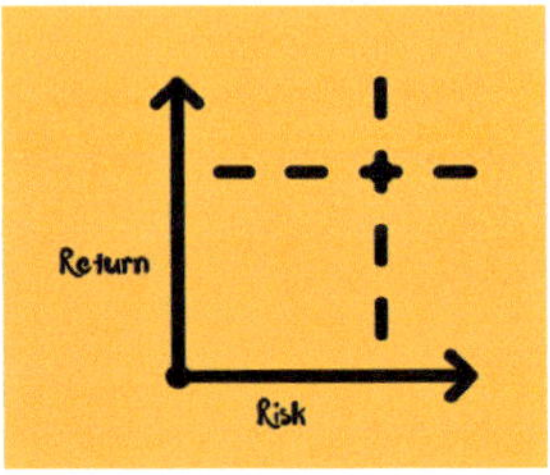

For high-risk tolerance, you can expect to make an above-average return. With low-risk tolerance, you can expect average returns on your investment, which should not be disappointing as you are taking on a lower level of risk.

Before we conclude, let's put some context around what average means. The average risk will be the risk of the "market," and the average return will be the return of the "market."

So if you invested in an S&P index, as we discussed in the previous chapter, the index's returns would be the average returns. Without going into technical jargon, the risk of the market is always = 1.

Risk and Returns are always intertwined. One can safely conclude that if an investment offers you unreasonable lucrative returns, it certainly comes attached with higher risk - whether you are told about it or not!

Get Educated, Know your Money and Invest Responsibly!

Risk vs Return

QUIZ

1. What is the measure of risk?

A.Trading Volumes
B. Earnings growth rate of a company
C. Volatility which measures how much the price swings up or down over a given period

2. Risk tolerance is

A. Situational
B. Psychological
C. Both

3. What is your willingness to take risks?

A. Your will to accept a loss if it occurs
B. Your will to trade stocks
C. Your preference to invest only in real estate

4. What is your ability to take risks?

A. To be able to have a broker invest for you
B. The size of your wealth that will allow for a loss if it does occur without jeopardizing your financial goals
C. To be able to hire a portfolio manager

5. What is the relationship between Risk and Return?

A. Risk is unavoidable. The higher the risk, the higher should be the return
B. Risk cannot be managed. You should accept any return irrespective of the risk
C. Risk & return are not related. One has nothing to do with the other

1.C | 2.C | 3.A | 4.B | 5.A

05

UNDERSTANDING DIVERSIFICATION

In the last lesson, you learned how to establish your risk tolerance and define realistic expectations of investment returns. In this lesson, we take it a step further to discuss how you can use diversification as a tool to align your investments to your risk tolerance.

What is diversification?

Diversification is a way to reduce the risk of your investment portfolio by spreading the risk.

An investment portfolio is a collection of all your investment like stocks, bonds, cryptocurrency, real estate, etc.

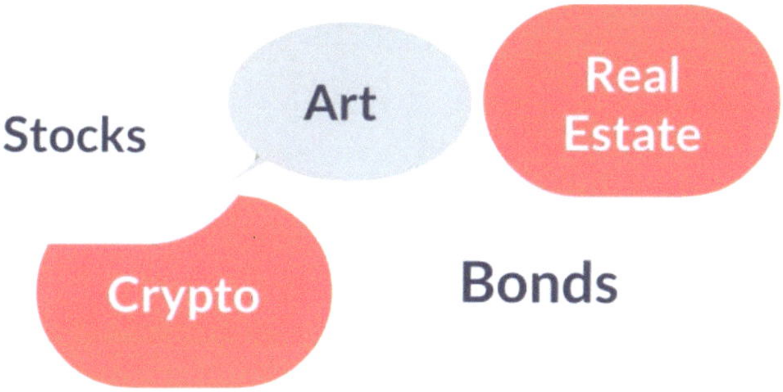

Concentration is the opposite of diversification, where you invest in one or two securities, thereby concentrating not only your investment but also your risk.

Comparing Portfolios

Let's look at two portfolios to understand the concept further.

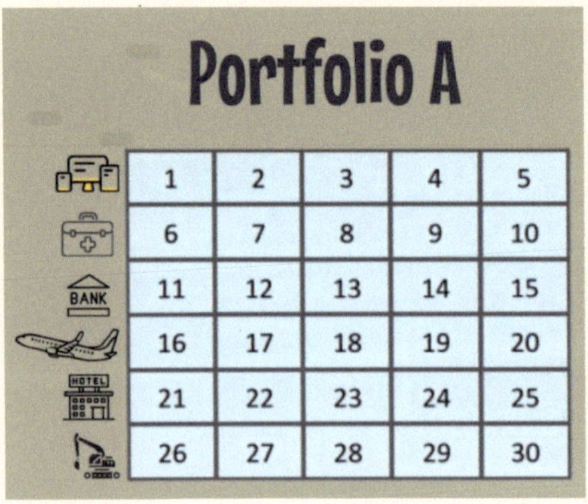

- Diversified portfolio
- Invested in 30 different stocks spread across 6 industries like tech, healthcare, banking, airlines, hotels, and construction.
- The risk of Portfolio A is the average risk of the 30 stocks

- Concentrated portfolio.
- Invested in just one stock of a technology company.
- The risk of Portfolio B is the risk of just one stock.

To lose your money on portfolio A, all 30 stocks across 6 industries will have to underperform simultaneously. However, only one stock has to lose its value for portfolio B, and the portfolio will begin to incur losses.

The example demonstrates your risk concentration and lack of diversification in portfolio B. Higher the risk, the higher the probability of a gain or a loss. On the other hand, Portfolio A will generally maintain a stable risk level and offer you average returns.

As we discussed in the previous chapter, risk and return go hand in hand. The return on these two portfolios will be pretty different.

When it comes to investing, the phrase "NOT putting all your eggs in one basket" cannot be more appropriate.

This becomes increasingly important as you age.

Your financial responsibilities increase, and not meeting your financial goals can have a more significant impact on the stability of your life.

Impact of Diversification

Diversification will not eliminate risk, meaning you can still lose money on some of your investments. Diversification will decrease the risk by spreading it. You may incur losses in one area but expect to be compensated in another.

The performance of your portfolio will depend on how good you are at picking stocks. Most of us are not - it is a skill and an art.

You can hire a portfolio manager/financial advisor or invest in a well-diversified fund on your own. Just remember to perform research on what you are investing in, including fees and tax implications.

What is Asset Allocation?

You can further diversify your portfolio by adding different asset classes.

Defining what asset classes you invest in is called Asset Allocation

Asset allocation reduces risks further as each asset class behaves differently in various economic situations. A portfolio with an asset allocation across bonds, stocks, real estate, and cryptocurrency will be more diversified than a portfolio with just stocks.

To summarize

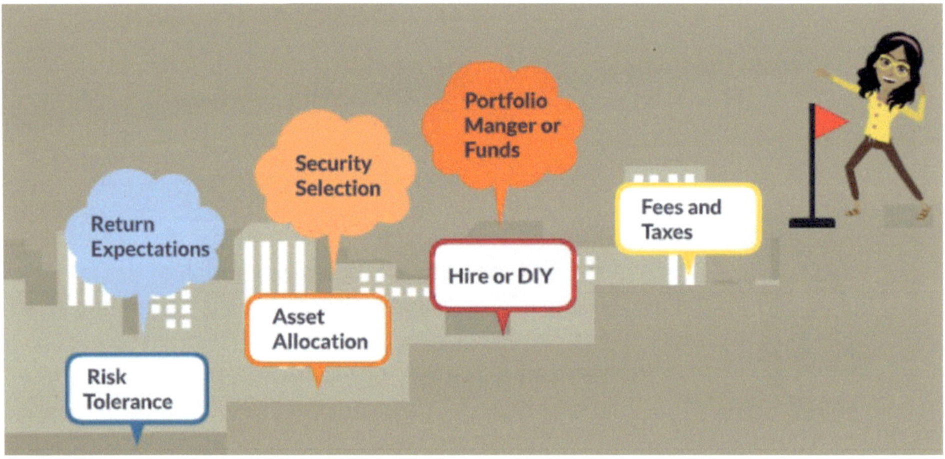

To tie it all together:

1. Start with your risk tolerance, which then defines your return expectations
2. Decide your asset allocation
3. Hire an expert, or invest in a well-diversified fund
4. Be mindful of all the fees and tax implications

Happy investing. Don't forget to invest responsibly!

Diversification

QUIZ

1. What is Portfolio Diversification?

A.Investing in a single stock
B. A way to reduce the risk of your overall investment portfolio by spreading the risk
C. Investing in a single company's bonds

2. What is Portfolio Concentration?

A. Investing in one or two securities thereby concentrating not only your investment but also your risk
B. Index Investing
C. Investing in Mutual Funds

3. What is asset allocation?

A. Allocating your savings in different bank accounts
B. Defining what asset classes you invest in
C. Allocating your expenses on different credit cards

4. Why does asset allocation reduce risk?

A. Because each asset class behaves differently in different economic situations
B. It invests in similar assets
C. It keeps money safe in the bank's saving account

5. What are the steps to start investing?

A. Invest all of your money to buy your favorite stock
B. Define risk tolerance, set return expectations, decide asset allocation, invest in diversified funds or hire a portfolio manager, and don't forget to do due diligence on fees & taxes
C. Ask friends for suggestions and begin trading on recommendations

1.B | 2.A | 3.B | 4.A | 5.B

06

MAKE YOUR FIRST TRADE

How to get started

We added a bonus lesson for those who do not know where to start. Here is a step-by-step guide to executing your first trade. You can skip this chapter if you already know how to trade.

1 Open a brokerage account

- Pick an established brokerage house like Fidelity, Ameritrade, Schwab, etc.
- Submit identification documents like SSN, license along with an application form for a brokerage account
- Additional documents may be required for options trading and requesting a margin account that allows you to trade using leverage.

Opening an account is very easy. Most accounts can be opened online.

2 Link your bank account and transfer money

- This is no different from linking your bank account to Paypal
- Transfer money to your brokerage account

Don't wait to collect a lot of money. Start with $10. Investing is a habit; the sooner you start, the better

3 Execute your first trade

- Decide you want to trade. You will need the ticker symbol, a unique code used to identify the stock. E.g., IVV is a ticker if you're going to invest in an S&P index ETF. Other details are as below:

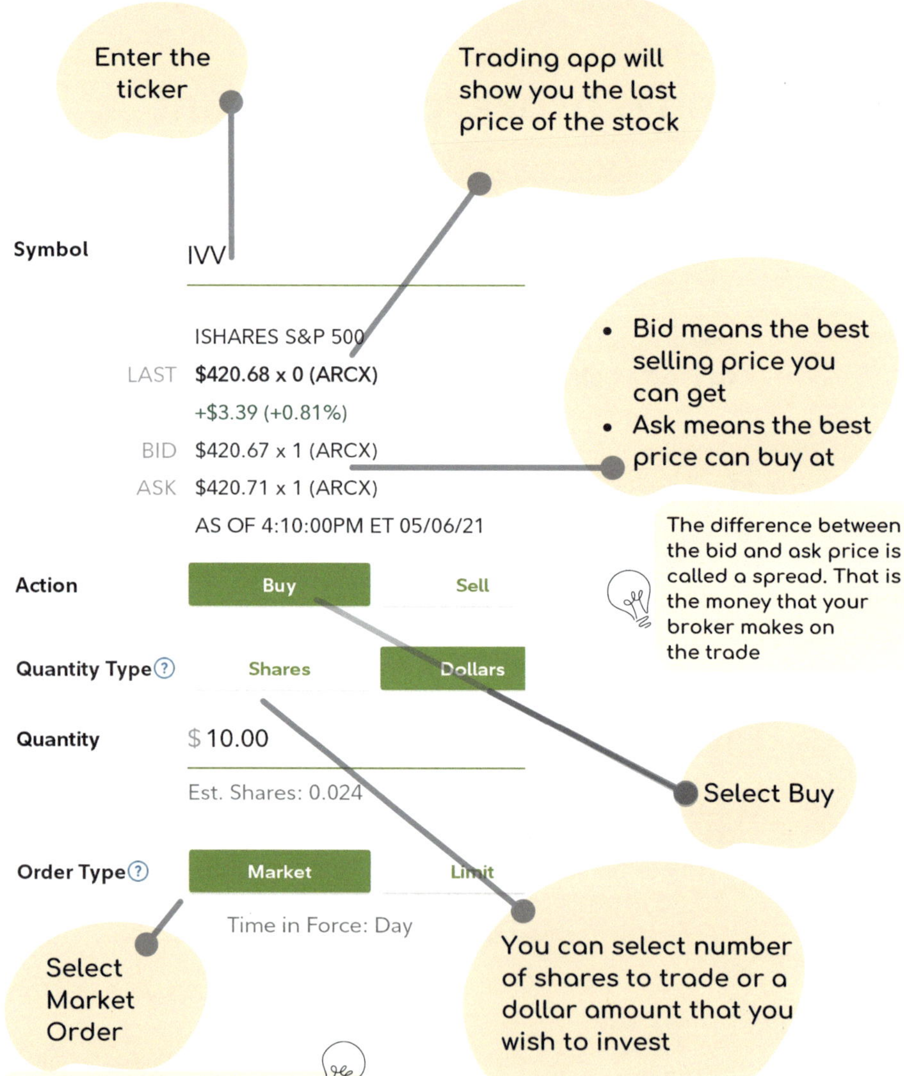

The difference between the bid and ask price is called a spread. That is the money that your broker makes on the trade

There are a lot of order types. You can research more on this topic. But for a retail buyer, a market order is good enough.

Words of caution

Before we conclude the book, below are some tips for when you first start trading.

- BE DISCIPLINED

Don't get swayed and influenced by meme stocks; remember the lesson on Risk and Return.

- SINGLE STOCK TRADES

It is challenging for an average investor to pick individual stocks and do better than the market. Remember that once you make a loss, your money has to work extra hard to make up for that loss and THEN work further to generate the lost returns. A stock's popularity is not a reason to buy; someone else's profit (or lucky strike) is not your loss.

- STAY AWAY FROM EXOTIC TRADES

Options trading is a very niche area and requires a particular skill set. Avoid getting into trades that you do not understand.

- AVOID MARGIN TRADING

Once you've built a decent portfolio, the brokerage company will offer an option to trade on margin, which is nothing more than a loan provided to you by the broker (your trading app) to buy more securities. The securities in your portfolio become collateral, and if you incur losses, the broker will have the right to sell your securities to protect their loan. Leverage trading is not recommended. Always trade as 'Cash' and not 'Margin.'

- INVESTING IN CRYPTOCURRENCY

All of the cryptocurrencies, including Bitcoin, are extremely risky. The prices fluctuate exponentially, and because they are new, it is impossible to predict the prospects of one specific currency. Regulations can change, the technology can evolve, governments can start to issue a cryptocurrency - all or any of which can significantly impact your investment. Additionally, there are no established principles to estimate the real value, making it harder to know the true worth of your investment. If you must, then make sure you invest only a fraction of your portfolio and only after you have established a rainy day fund.

Other content from the author

THE ILLUSTRATED BOOK OF MONEY MANAGEMENT

Learn fundamental topics of money management:

1. Know your paycheck
2. Budgeting
3. Banking
4. Credit Explained
5. Protecting Identity
6. Know your taxes
7. Inflation
8. Compounding Explained

Order it on our website www.fiwe.app/the-book

DOWNLOAD THE FIWE APP

- Access all lessons as animated videos
- Available on Apple and Play store

CONTACT

@fiweapp

support@fiweapp

Building wealth is a slow, disciplined, and long-term process.

There is no getting rich quick strategy. It's your money - get educated and invest responsibly.

Happy Investing!

Made in the USA
Monee, IL
05 November 2026

67988164R00024